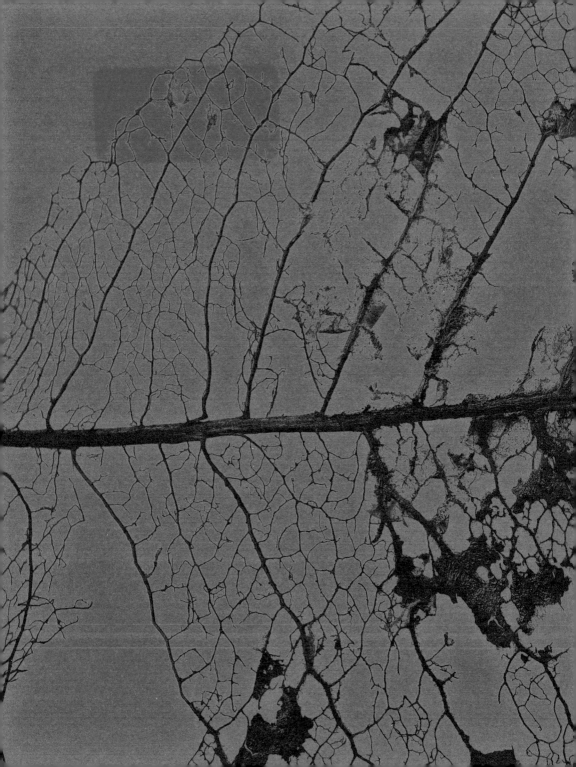

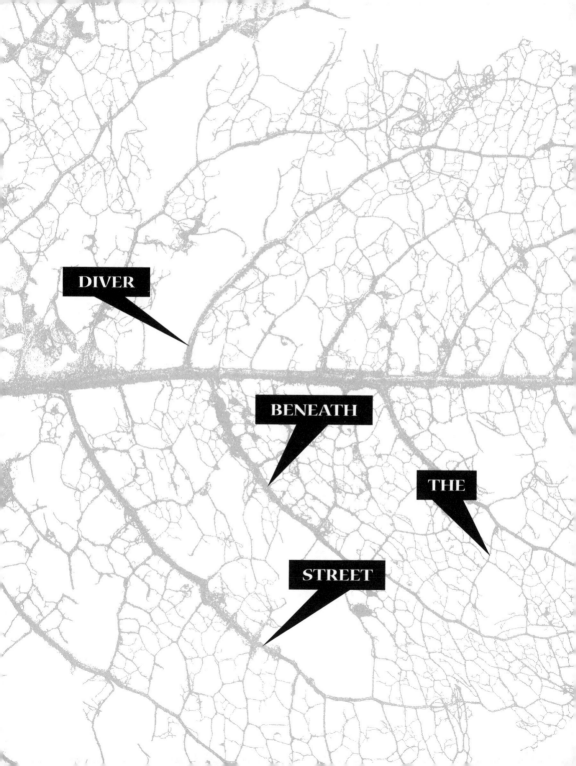

Praise for
Diver Beneath the Street

"Petra Kuppers's *Diver Beneath the Street* knows we're no safer asleep in our beds than straying from the path into the forest or taking to the streets. *Me too,* whisper its poems from under the factory-desecrated ground, where twelve princesses don their masks and a whole mycelium network lights up the dance floor. In this bold book, fairy tale becomes rallying cry, true crime becomes true rhyme, murder mystery becomes cosmic mysticism, and wreckage becomes wonder."
—**Danielle Pafunda, author of** *Along the Road Everyone Must Travel*, **winner of the Saturnalia Books Poetry Prize**

"What happens when the murder house is down the street? When grim fairy tales are true? With vivid language and visceral wit, Petra Kuppers dives into the wreckage of poisoned ecologies: violence, geography, and nature. Come drift here across ley lines into beetle and bone, axe and sap. Come dance the earth séance of virus and white pine elixir. This book is a reliquary, a remediation, a gift: 'a blossom to honor the dead.'"
—**Gabrielle Civil, author of** *the déjà vu: black dreams & black time*

"There are many voices that arise from the natural world that call us to attention. But there are none as clear, as vital, or as important as that of Petra Kuppers. In *Diver Beneath the Street*, Kuppers serves as a doula for ghosts and landscapes and illuminates, like a searchlight trapped in the pandemic's lighthouse, the intricate and often devastating connections binding violence, terrain, and the feminine form. *Diver Beneath the Street* will live in your bones."

—**CMarie Fuhrman**, coeditor of *Cascadia Field Guide: Art, Ecology, Poetry* and *Native Voices: Indigenous American Poetry, Craft and Conversations*

"Kuppers's poetic language is agile and rich, dynamic and beautiful, but Kuppers also places the evocative quality of language within the realm of injustice, violence, and community upheaval. *Diver Beneath the Street* feels like quite a careful and thoughtful juxtaposition of both joy and horror, which culminates in an assertion of survival."

—**Ginger Ko**, author of *POWER ON*

"Pushing off from Adrienne Rich's 'Diving into the Wreck,' Petra Kuppers swims around under the pavement, where sexual terror seeps into body and soil and the poisons of real fairy-tale nightmares supercharge the old trope of woman as landscape. Yet Kuppers reveals natural models for healing and finds solace in our vast, collective imaginations. If this enthralling and revelatory book doesn't reorient you toward the subterrain and the subaltern, toward deep feminist ecologies, what will?"

—**Christine Hume**, author of *Everything I Never Wanted to Know*

Diver

Beneath the Street

Poems by
Petra Kuppers

Wayne State University Press
Detroit

MADE IN MICHIGAN WRITERS SERIES

GENERAL EDITORS
Michael Delp, Interlochen Center for the Arts
M. L. Liebler, Wayne State University

A complete listing of the books in this series can be found
online at wsupress.wayne.edu.

ISBN 9780814351116 (paperback)
ISBN 9780814351123 (e-book)

Library of Congress Control Number: 2023944739

Cover image © HHelene / Shutterstock. Cover design by Brad Norr Design.
Image description: a neon-green skeleton leaf's botanical lace lances downward
into earth. Beneath the word *Diver*, a horizon melts brown
into black. Red labels speak of maps and crime scenes.

Publication of this book was made possible by a generous gift
from The Meijer Foundation.

Wayne State University Press rests on Waawiyaataanong, also referred to as Detroit,
the ancestral and contemporary homeland of the Three Fires Confederacy. These
sovereign lands were granted by the Ojibwe, Odawa, Potawatomi, and Wyandot Nations,
in 1807, through the Treaty of Detroit. Wayne State University Press affirms Indigenous
sovereignty and honors all tribes with a connection to Detroit. With our Native
neighbors, the press works to advance educational equity and promote
a better future for the earth and all people.

Wayne State University Press
Leonard N. Simons Building
4809 Woodward Avenue
Detroit, Michigan 48201-1309

Visit us online at wsupress.wayne.edu.

In Memoriam

Mary Terese Fleszar

Joan Elspeth Schell

Maralynn Skelton

Dawn Louise Basom

Jane Mixer

Alice Elizabeth Kalom

Karen Sue Beineman

Roxie Ann Phillips

Annetta Nelson

Nancy Harrison

Travesene Ellis

Tamara Jones

Deborah Reynolds

Contents

. . . string of murders on the east side
—another woman's . . . is found in a vacant house.
"She was wrapped up in a carpet," [her sister]
(*FOX 2 Detroit*, 2019) . . . targeted . . .
in their 50s . . . derelict houses (*Washington Post*, 2019)

In 1967 . . . time of peace, free love, hitchhiking, nineteen-year-old

. . . walking home . . . apartment in Ypsilanti

. . . partially buried . . . abandoned farm . . .
six more . . . female students.
(Edward M. Keyes, *The Michigan Murders*, 1976)

evidence . . . came from a home owned . . . in Ypsilanti.
. . . Before they left for vacation . . .

wife gave his kids haircuts in the basement.
The clippings . . . swept . . . piles . . . left. (*FOX 2 Detroit*,
fiftieth anniversary of killings, 2019)

It almost looks like you take a nice piece of lace,
and you lay it down over the lung. . . .
That's actually
the scarring around the air sacs.
(Gaetane Michaud, chief of interventional pulmonology at NYU Langones
Perlmutter Cancer Center, about COVID-19, *WTSP 10 Tampa Bay*, 2021)

Compass: A Preface

Will you dive with me, explore the wreck, with creatures and spirits, inside and out, toward dissolve?

This book began once upon a time, in 2011, when I picked up a tattered paperback, *The Michigan Murders*, from the free shelves of the Ann Arbor Public Library. I began reading it while traveling with my wheelchair on the bus to the Detroit airport.

Once upon a time, and many many times before and after, this land tasted blood. Women, trans, and queer people have died and die by men's violence, all in unequal precarity in a racist world.

From 1967 to 1969, in Ann Arbor and Ypsilanti, a serial killer murdered white women, most of them students. He picked them up as they traveled to parties, to libraries, to the lakes; left them on roadsides, in gullies, on construction sites, in old barns.

Money runs in new ways through automotive industries. Toxic runoff trickles below the factory floor. Capitalist giants stamp new neighborhoods out of the rural land.

Here I make my fairy-tale home, speak with the White Pine, dance at Ypsi Pride. The murder house is just down the street.

> Where was I? I was born a queer in 1968 in a small village in Germany.
>
> Where was she? I picture photos of my mother, a few years before my birth. She never finished high school, never went to a university town, never toward the open.
>
> Where does Rumpelstilzchen live?

The old tale keeps spinning. In 2019, a serial killer murdered older Black women and left them in abandoned homes in Detroit. I drive by, on my way to performance sites where I work. Crime tape, evening news, hurtful words, tearful sisters, angry lump in my stomach, bear witness.

Once upon a time, the tale changed for everybody: access to space constricted during the COVID-19 lockdown. The virus dove into me in March 2020, shook me badly, constricted my own air. I wrote and wrote during the global shelter-in-place, in an animate clusterfucked fairy-tale world.

Between horror and the soil's plenitude: Let's break it down, let it run with the waters of the Giwitatigweiasibi, the Huron River. Burn and recycle the story, reclaim nutrients below the Roundup-neon lawns. Reconstruct between the six lips of the nematode out hunting with the springtails, with the beetles, beneath the raven's caw.

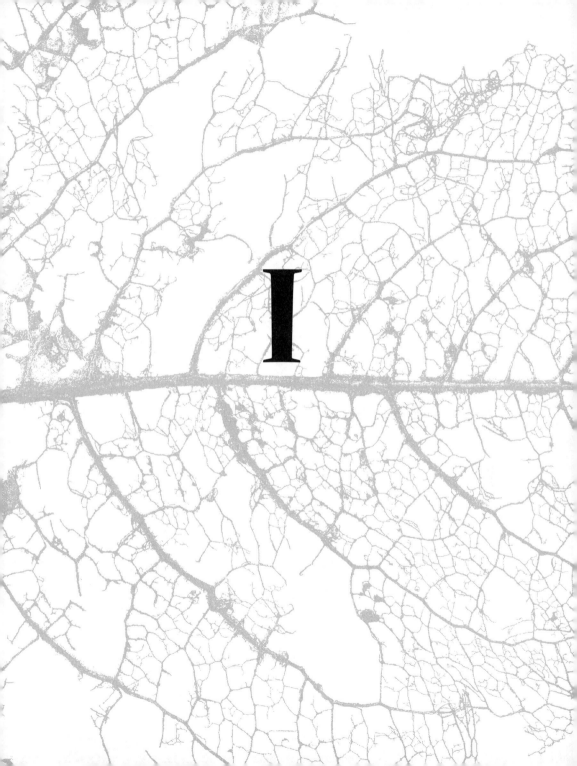

I

The Diver Beneath the Street

The diver sucks the sugar cube, goes under.

Huron pinches her waist.

She dives.

Giant wet tongue kiss full of moss and foul tree juice.

Oil smears above her head.

If I tell the truth, I am the diver.
If I tell the truth, these women have been dead for as long as I have been alive.
If I tell the truth, there's the visceral thrill of her skipping along the railway
line where the Amtrak runs, the last glimpse, the beret on top of her head, her
thoughts on her school exam, a gumball stuck in her teeth.

I do not see the dark wave pulling her under, the car, the man, black hair and
leather, sun-kissed skin.

The diver sinks deeper into the muck.

Sugar blood.

Her hands are busy searching in the darkness.

Her visibility is nil.

There are plastic-bag ghosts drifting, drifting.

If I tell the truth, the river has swallowed.
If I tell the truth, let's slide into the dive along the right swerve of the lane.
If I tell the truth, I dream of a motorcycle wheel with a necklace braided into
the spokes.

Rust moths filter tanning chemicals.
Wing crystals.

I scry the round mouth

    on the underside of the water's limit:

        here she cried in truth.

Now the   waters   rise
                      every year.

The diver sees the street beneath

    the water,

      flipper curls

        mud up

          from broken asphalt.

She shoots up.

    Exits through the marsh curtain.

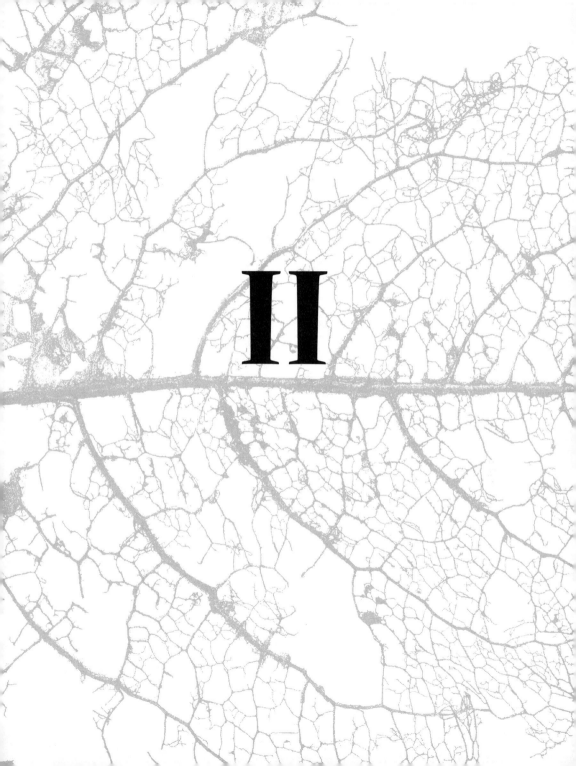

II

Dancing Princesses

An unknown number of princesses vanish at night. They go down a trapdoor
in their bedrooms, sisters all. The hole in the ground leads to a winding path.
The path enters a silver forest. Then a golden forest. Then a forest of diamonds.
The detective who follows them in an invisibility cloak breaks a bough.
The trees scream.

The unknown number of princesses arrive at a lake. An unknown number of
princes and princesses await them with boats. They hitch a ride, and the invisible
detective jumps in with the youngest princess. Her swain complains that the boat
is heavier than normal. The princess says,

"It's the heat. We are all getting tired."

The company arrives at a castle. They dance the night away. At 3 a.m., the shoes of
an unknown number of princesses are worn through.

In tatters, with holes, decayed and fragile.

They all, including the invisible detective, run home, up the staircase, through the
trapdoor, across the creaky floorboards, and are found asleep the next morning.

*

There were two brothers by the name of Grimm. They collected this tale. A story
brought to them. Sometimes unnamed women garnered the stories. Detectives at
the hearth. Informants.

Ethnographic practices in the German countryside. Fantasy police procedural.

To warn of the dire wolf. To not go out at night. To see your true true love in a
lying mirror. To dance in burning coals. *Wesens* live all around you right now.

In the Grimms' story, the detective is an old, tired soldier, out to gain a wife and a kingdom if he finds the answer to the vanishing women and their danced-out shoes.

There are few answers, and only a handful that would stand up in court.

In this story. Numbers are not endless. Numbers huge and obscured. Detectives hurt others in their hunt. Trees scream with the train whistle.

This poem could be printed on a piece of old T-shirt, worn and velvet from washing and from the rain. Maybe a mouse pilfers threads for its nest. A swallow shits on it, coming home into the barn's high beams after hunting and eating a thick furry moth.

*

Women vanish, are accused of going dancing.

Kings and queens alert them to danger and seek to imprison them with heavy door locks and golden keys.

The danger comes from the soldiers out there. Good citizens blend in to fool. The youngest princess, not fourteen years old, climbs into her ride.

A boat of a car, fins slice the air, traverse the moat, the princess so dark so fair.

In the night.

Sleep in the golden bough. Sleep in the abandoned lot.

Diamond eyelids blink cat's eyes for the club.

Lies to the mother.

There lies the rub.

The Candyman brings the dope. The rope swings in the barn. The neighbors spin the yarn.

Rumpelstilzchen should be recognizable, that's all they ask for, like a hunchback in an Identi-Kit.

Clouds vanish in the clear-cut lantern jaw.

The maw of suburbia.

Reintegration

> She has difficulty writing, even imagining, that girl—that girl's body, her life, what she might have been feeling.
>
> —Donna de la Perrière, *Works of Love & Terror*

Beetle transports human hair to its burrow.
It's down, she's down. Hair nests deep beneath

earth. Long black hairs, loosened, wound
around adhesive footpads—pulvilli—

welcome to a new home of soil-based grease.
Lawn care feelings echo the earth's rotation.

Sunshine warms the entry hole till it glows.
Deep beetle sees the round ahead, a gloriole, a halo.

Beetle saints drip tiny bits of hair, towheaded child's
clippings become plush fillings for larvae featherbeds.

Grass verge feels the trap between the cambium's
pure water: tree feels effluvia, flow in progress, suck.

Black paint dappled onto green leaf feelings, rosy glow.
Road divider wild plant feelings: grass kneels down.

Tree umbrellas with the widest arms reach to neighbor.
Shade and scorch releases fluids. Cadaverine particles soak

into clay, bind with kaolin that bakes into whiteness.
Grass feels pressure when a line of policemen tramp.

Tree falls   after the arson fire   jumps over the barn,   into its arms.
Grass feels the impact this time: heavy.   It booms.

This is no casual throw, no careful positioning.   This hurts.
Mud churns milk-like from earth and rain,   shoe ballet mashes

wine grapes,   chlorophyll juices squelch   into a broth.
Sparrow jumps into shoe print.   Worms sing round *Os*.

Dark world pecks them   into twos,   each survives, thrives,
deeply tucked   into narrow tunnels of clay-cool earth.

Touch the worm's hind part,   galvanize taste buds,
signal the feast.   Blowflies land in aromatic clouds.

Tastes of salt leach far,   ring crystals spread a root bale.
Bloat and release: the bubble sinks to the sigh of leaves.

Shift phosphorus bioavailability.   Change graphs.
Use asphalt to neutralize the last nitrogen,   fix it into soil,

Find the ancient photograph,   tender skins baked deep,
before spring rain can wash it into the river.

Feed algae bloom,

    a blossom to honor the dead.

Fungi Moves

Deciduous pincers close in over winter. Tulips push
against earth knot, fangs break surface. Origami folds rise
into March light. Narcissi spy with their yellow eyes.
Dark-rooted grip lifts a dogwood arc above the brick.
Pink blossoms rain down dandruff in premature spring.
Kitty-corner, vampiristic yard tree chomps to join
corseted sugar maples that hint of reddish stance.
Mats of Kentucky bluegrass creep along southern border,
annex mycelium strands to weave a secret glucose code.
Dense nutrients shuttle deep below grind undeterred by
orderly peony plugs that will shake and shake come April.

Michigan Murders

What will it be, a figment
of your imagination?

—Maggie Nelson, *Jane: A Murder*, a quote attributed to her grandfather,
part of Nelson's poetry/memoir about her aunt Jane, who was long
presumed to have been killed by the Michigan Murderer.

Ghosts on every street corner. Dinosaur roars into the
four-square night. It's the year after the Algiers Motel.
Every ten years, another field succumbs to a street name.
In the large city, a house dies quietly, then the next.

Ypsilanti night terrors. Women on a thumb. Women on
the dump. Women down the basement stairs. Women
in the laundry room.

I follow the maps, chart the green swale's rhythm.
Parcels of brown quadrangle the clay. Huron River
watershed kisses its wider bed. Swamp ground. Ride
your bicycle: the city looms to the east, past the water
tower, into the rising sun.

Blanket spread. Backyards lean into one another, a pole,
a metal grid, the air. The depth of a dog's run. Rusty
swings hidden behind privacy fence. A thin line of
debris marks the last flood.

Tree crowns notched into a V by DTE, power bite.

On Labor Day, we assemble in the house two doors
down, bring chocolate-tofu cake with raspberries
and eat spinach dip like it's 1973. Star Wars ice cream,
storm trooper fudge nuggets and toffee swirl. Around
the table, dementing men nod with smiling faces.
Remember the news.

Weave the net of care: listen, be listened to, exchange perspectives on the local nursing homes, but in the end, we have them near.

Near to me. Near to Washtenaw Ave. Near to the club. Near to the bar. Near to the hairdresser and wigmaker, have a new hairpiece, change it up.

You are only young once, and the night beckons and Ann Arbor's wild dance.

The wigmaker does not like the look of him. The wigmaker does not like the leather men. The stink and the roar. The wigmaker talks to the salesgirl. Don't hitch that ride.

The bullfrog croaks between the properties, this side, then that side, jumps over the barely developed line. Cedar shingles lap over the tiles.

You can go to the vintage car shows in Depot Town, fins slice the air in slo-mo, bustle pride, leather wipe. Bubble-gum colors no longer factory original. Would you like to have a ride on my Naugahyde? 1969 Oldsmobile Cutlass, red and white, pristine condition, well swabbed.

In my house, in the cellar. I hum into the air, trace the ley lines. There was a pentagram here. The neighbors didn't tell us, didn't want to scare us off. Men in regalia run rites in the garden. The son of the house writes etiquette books for pagan gatherings.

Ley lines reach across the fence and into the street, to the dimmer parts away from the noise of Washtenaw Avenue. Deep backyards. The river comes and nibbles up the drains. Ice cream sticks to my craw, the rhododendron crinkle brown at the paper's edge.

The Ypsilanti auto plant worker is excused from the jury. "*I don't think it would be fair for me to be a juror at this trial. I could not do him justice.*"

The sheep of the Michigan morning eat the clover from the lawn. Send you out to pasture. Over the railway line, to the burned shed.

The bar vibrates with the arresting news. They compare the photos in the paper. They roar up the road.

I call on the powers of the east. The powers of the morning sun. The squirrel nibbles on the ragged cloth caught in the cemetery's fence, out Superior Township way.

The motorist climbs out of her car. Something caught her eye, she says. Something winked out there. Remember me. Remember her.

The dial ray returns, glints off a shard of glass by the side of the road, off the muted sign, bulbs burned out, hits the seeds of garden flowers, rows upon rows, before the tiny cellar window.

New owners change the direction of the house. It looks out to the west now, the evening, a cardinal jewel in the violets of polluted air. The west will set you free. Thunderbird roars from the power engine's sinking, sinking sun.

The washing machine vibrates in the night, black paint stains creep up the stairs. The chalk of the circle twitches like a compass needle. The skunk crosses the line.

She stands and looks out of the portal, feet planted firmly among the purple coneflowers. A home of matches, ready to flare. A home of squirrels, doves in the air.

I stop the car. A home of weeds that hum along energy lines, copper connects, do not break the circuit. Make a quick buck, rip out the line, de-cultivate. I follow.

Vacant directions: the sun shines through the slats of the barn, through carpet fibers where the mice rake debris to make their nest.

Viral Crime

When you really want an ice cream sundae,
green peepers swamp, fungi poof smell.

Slouched in. Roof caved in. Raked through the mud.
Lampshade baked into orange flocked wallpaper.

Disinfect the mail. Cover your relations.
Emotions are produced in the body as sensation

interpreted by the brain. Don't inhale too much.
Make sure the sanitizer rain has time to kill

any bacteria that might
have been introduced

during the mixing
    mixing process.

Blunt force trauma. Yogurt, bananas, sunshine.
True crime rendered. On the swing set, a brooch

partakes of the nature of both speech and song.
Worm eats in the tender armpit, leg fascia stretch.

Alphabetize your books today, use the nib
sleeve to rub away dust. Sneeze sinus, find

action of cutting off a person's or animal's limbs.
A recommended sewing pattern, along with

retch until the rib cage dislocates,
suggested carpet materials,

look down at the soil,
can never ever

be found,
look down at the soil.

Coventry Street, Detroit

The black mold fungus Stachybotrys chartarum *was originally discovered on the wall of a house in Prague in 1837. The average person inhales at least forty conidia (fungus spores) per hour.*

Action.

I zoom into the vulnerable opening, quiver shot.
Curb is a bump, tender green clad, a carpet thick,
dry patches, razor burn. Over the occluded lines
of sidewalk, grey engraving into riotous weeds.
Sun shines on my back, birdsong in the city,
world smells open, rain-fresh, steaming.
My lens finds the first stoop.

Cut.

Pan to the banister, peel, skin flakes, dry,
long strips, old paint emulsified: durable metal,
lead resists moisture for a time, now fragment,
fly, get away, fly with the wind, disseminate, go.

Action.

Sneakered foot crashes through splintery wood.
Rebalance. A teenager's locks billow
into my view finder.
Crash's echo finds bird-wing beat, beat
inside, craw clamor.

Cut.

A heavy lock, red rusty closed hasp, over
medium-density plywood, door-shaped,
window-shaped, anchored against release.

Action.

A mold spore winks through the crack between
the crumbly window frame and new board,
angles at a cocky tilt into the wind.
Cellulose-sated, the fungus spore twirls, scents,
drifts toward damp, the open, and slips
with heaving sigh down toward inner
tree, branches welcome, to tiny end points,
round apples wet and shaken with oxygen's
embrace. It binds itself to the wall, a painting,
memory of a home, nods on its growing stalk.

Cut.

Camera on the back of teenager on the move,
laughter peals in my ears, race to next
delivery station.

Tree Trimming on Roosevelt Street

Upon drifting along Roosevelt Street, the street where I live, near the house that was the site of the last known Ypsilanti murder.

Colonial pockets of privacy fencing parcel the trees.
Concrete tattoos on the river floodplain.

Crunchy leaves of early winter carpet the row.
Clog the roof drains with pine needle pick-up sticks.

Rainwater transformation of sugars into resin pearls.
Roots knit up around the water lines, strangle the flow.

Rat hairs condition the soil, organ meats deliquesce to juice.
Raccoon and groundhog stink defeats the convivial deck.

Intricate leaf skeletons aggregate into suburban compost.
If I do not disturb the layers, charcoal rings mark the passing.

Influx of copper, in my birth year, nourishes tree roots, part of the rot.
If no humans were here, the soil level would rise half an inch in fifty years.

Morning-time, pin of pain wakes me to protest the tree cutters' crane.
Moss wraps around dead tree limbs, game crews hack to the bone.

Maples are tender along the street plumb, a disease of home.
Marrow sucked from the deep, time in flow.

Electricity lines sway in the remaining V of tree crowns.
Even now, as pecked from above so below.

Elevations drain ley lines to the Huron River.
Ectoplasmic veils evaporate over dense old soil.

Orderly Street Ghost

> The soil of graves is the transformer.
> —William Bryant Logan, *Dirt: The Ecstatic Skin of the Earth*

burn glitter into the tree root
wave a curvy perm into the frost
sparkle the lawn like a pony in heat
roots twine around your fingerbone
deep in the hollow, deep hollow earth
basement level end station
shovel falls into rust debris

walk on

hairs prickle my neck tendrils deep
brown flecks on the laundry room floor
paint, so much paint, glitter
solar lights, tree boughs,
do not cover you up
do not cover you
burn memory root

walk on

on the sidewalk I douse for
depth channel vibration
in the culvert, for white clowns,
for deadly motorcycles, cut hair
souvenirs, not curling
iron taste buds stilled
under his glittering knife

walk on

specter, blank leather soled,
finger trail in spiky skeletons
rattlesnake master
iris weeps along the path
dogwood blood
do not step on the crack
do not break a woman's back

walk on

Night Crawlers

Roseate snow billows into storm
willow weeps rings of Saturn dissolve

moonlight spills out of the glassless bay window
downward, downward, bores magic into the ground.

My footstep hits hard, dies buzzy in kneecap's hollow,
worms faint into femur head. Hard stop. Arrest.

Worm tunnels freeze to stiff pockets beneath,
beetle carapaces folded to deep winter tent.

Crawl energy zaps a house-height beneath me,
no rain, no snow, no wind, no sun, no hail, no fog

lights worm cavern, winter vacuum beneath slime.
Sleep in the winter, ball in jellied umbra:

bind us deep down, fix nitrogen, seed soils,
clasp hard memories of liquid earthen spring.

Linnhurst, Between Gratiot and Chambers, Detroit

Plans are under way to board up vacant structures within a mile radius of the three locations where the women's bodies were found," [Detroit Mayor] Duggan's chief of staff Alexis Wiley said Thursday.
    —George Hunter, "Possible serial murders shine light on Detroit's vacant homes," *The Detroit News*, June 7, 2019

Head on, I drive past a parking lot.

Next, a demolished factory.

Empty lot.

House. Blue paint.

Long empty lot, vegetation years old, reaching to the sun.

Sunshine smell, tree smell, grass smell. Old weed.

Recently demolished house, foundation still visible as chalk lines.

Three houses tight together, porches angled out into the sun.

Peoria Avenue.

A large house, red.

Two beautiful trees.

Six houses, an enclave together, cars in the driveway.

Open.

Two houses with cars.

No one is in the street.

I am honoring her steps.

She is alien to me.

There is time, and there is space, strata, terrain, terror.

This is a sparse, toothless story.

There are dusty city flowers.

This is a drive-by story, a stranger story, a momentary halt.

I am not drifting.

I will not be here at night.

There was the moon, in April, and beneath it, the tops of trees.

Porch boards moaned and splintered if you stepped wrong.

This was not a shelter, just a place out of view.

There is nothing to see here now.

Then, it was "staged," face down, spread to liquid, used condom.

There are flowers, at some times of the year.

Moonscapes of asphalt, driven up, volcanoes erupt.

The year they found her in that house, city police searched 3,000 abandoned properties.

Lay the copper lines of 3,000 homes together.

How far will you circle the earth?

Beneath the soil, a salt mine.

Salt, and bones, and copper, and the earth's blood.

Candy Cane Park

Twelve-year-old Carolyn King hit a ball in Ypsilanti's Candy Cane Park in 1973, defying the Little League's international ban on girls. The park dedicated to her abuts Roosevelt Street.

Two kids scream at the far end of Candy Cane Park. Yaw space between yellow teeth just right for slips onto the mauve-cushioned tongue.

He (for it was him, tight groin) hung on fleet feet mellow in the bushes.

White-beige skin drove down onto the motorcycle seat, jeans chafe wrinkles into dinosaur skin.

Randy Lane, behind the hydrangeas, just a yard or four before tree fangs guard a willow.

A screeching owl bites into neighborhood dusk.

He farts a roar, smooths metal downward toward extremities silver and blue, shoes touch rubber.

He feels the heat. And bellows golden flares to win her gaze.

She turns, steps halfway toward those kids, shopping bag a nest of spider's eggs.

She pivots. He rolls his wrist.

Sounds pierce, lag in the rider's ears.

He drowns in eyes; insect globes fracture the night at sunset.

He mounts lower in the saddle. Beast sheds its robes on the asphalt. Two eyes blink slow. Tongue turns in his maw.

Where she stood, where she labored, a net favors a bigger spider.

Exhaust fills up beast's lungs.

A dirty pearl in the park's dog dung, his tie rips before a giant scissors' wide and heavy stance.

Foundation Ore

Lead pours deep molten core.

Explode volcanic.

Scald skin, scald memory child, deep in the well. Child, shrivel fire hair, foresee new futures in the flame.

Create a culvert under the road. Canal. Run the rest.

Lead pours mobile, widening, eats the banks of body, artery, tissue field, eats till curve contained in cooling ooze.

Duct. Find local materials to create a bridge over the water's path.

Blood barrier. Brain barrier. Lay a pipe. Offer flood control. Gutter.

Lick the wall paint, white dust bedazzles the crib. Let the moisture drain. Spillway.

Avoid foundation damage. Lead chips a holey wall, a lacy fringe, plumb diary.

Notch doorpost.

Stick smeary black-and-white photograph between the battens of breathing walls.

Channel the path of excess away from buildings. Back to the mainstream. Sluice.

Lead bullets into grey mass, displace with splatter velocity, ping off clanging pipes, indoor plumbing.

No footprint on the dewy grass in the early morning. No chalky moon glimmers on new metals.

Suspend astronaut helmet crystals at night.

Lead glances at earth, at spine, at sky.

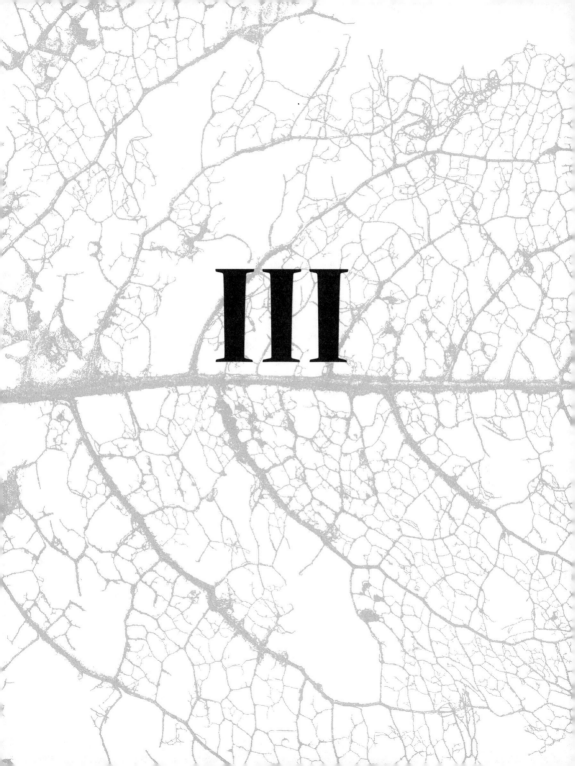

III

Tunnels

Each movement of respiration encodes terror.

—Stacy Doris, *Knot*

\

Muscle tunnel locomotive round, inmates held
      at psychiatric institutions

      Martín Ramírez sings rip-like architectures of invasion   invagination
holey fantasy scene in the mountain's side   Jesus's wound
     lay your finger here Thomas does as he is bidden
                    I, Thomasina, run for the hills

\   \   \

Underwater
cave. Mask
sound. Breath
beat. Cave
snake beneath
earth, stone
slick with
underwater
aquifer teaser
testers held at
bay but glide
right into the
next nest, one
h o l l o w
b e n e a t h

swallows   of
giant   gullet,
vocal   chords
tight against
neoprene
black

\

Dinosaur bone sticks out of desert cave wall high up
in the dry. Silicate old clay body sedimented fern.
Skin bird balances on hot wind. Giant stalagmites
bite into swampy dry sun parch heat death dinosaur
rattle roar tongue sail breath dust fall decay I salt
you here I bless you here I compress you here till

you reach   up in wide arc

        jubilation

\

The train comes round the mountain   spews a cigar is not a cigar   my muscles
anchor themselves   on bio-bones that stamp me a woman
osteoporosis work jumps up jumps up jumps strength
            cunt into elephant's maw   penile tusks
            the lioness's bloody fur clumps matted dirty to the ocher ground

        \   \

Breathing
apparatus
bangs noisily
yank   clank
funk   till   it
stops. Caught
lengthwise,
anchored.
Muscles seize
with ceiling at
nose. Beneath
the axle sharp
arrowtips fillet
skin fat
cushion. Sight
blurs red and
silt   and   silt
caught in fin
swirl. Stuck.

\\

Shark senses blood ampullae cruises into cave bung hole
fin delicacy convulses impale scar tumor tail and upper
fin stick out of sand till time falls away skeleton time
drip a mantle moan of liquid alabaster soapy skin.

Cave breath   vibrates animate

holes in the universe\\\

Fire scars pink into my flank   I scream   tunnel fills with water
till it pops teeth strain out plant matter and old silt
explodes downward, hummingbird diaphragm
lily-stems in the blood pool
blossom my heavy ovary

\\\

Shallow
breath louder
in the inner
ear, orchestra
c o r p u s c l e s
beat it beat it.
Flippers still.
Neoprene
shifts slightly
w   i   t   h
m o v e m e n t
side to side.
Rock   clasps
harder as lung
refuses to let
go.

\\\

She falls apart, memory of her, silk skin water hole
wedding dance, heavy pink feathers. Lake water

open, cool, each sucking wave. Deck dance against
desert dry alkaline water hole. Flames up, petrol

blue   a hot suck

                    gone.

\\

           \\\

Ball drops   tunnel takes glottal   stop all the way
            to bottom   impact   wave
rolls over me silver
            ball bearing high arc

\\

           \\\

                                              The   next
                                              b r e a t h .
                                              Bubbles in the
                                              aqueous
                                              humor of your
                                              eye,   death's
                                              sequins,
                                              m e r m a i d
                                              c o m p a n i o n

animals sprint
across   retina,
reflex shutter,
Morse   code
SOS.

\\\\   \\

She rattles hollow spirit anchor
arms wide. Low quake tsunami
fire press granite grind bones
contort till they flare into
cathedral ship. In the dry, dust

falls moth peacock scales.

Flame out giant turtle.

Farewell cave bear.

\\\\
                    \\

\   *To source.*   \

        \   \Stilled.   \

\ \Perfume molecules perform

memory leaps. \

\

\

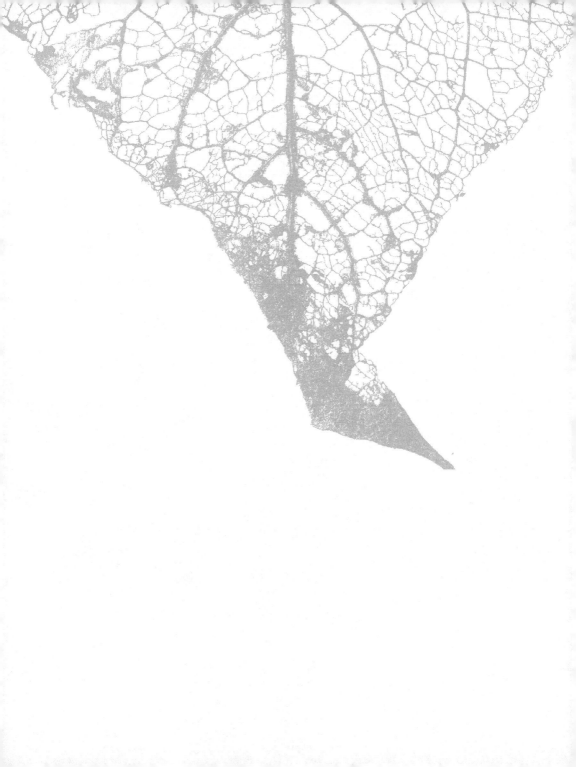

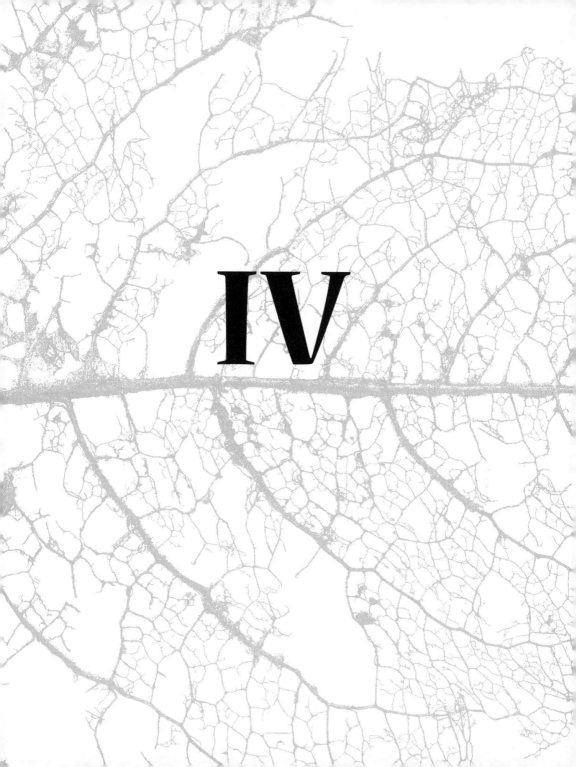

Night Dive

Painkillers: please soar and soak my stomach's lining,
drench, dissolve in acid, spread lake-like deep

inside, sink to shallow pool, roiled by spasms, muscles
in weak revolt. Then nerves lie fallow, capped, broken

small veins in my cheek, around my nose, sun damaged
childhood, coconut oil scent and heat like a blanket

fort, young birch tree caress in my soft hand, grass,
beetle, crumbs of earth spill brown, last moisture hint

licks sun, ancient star's heat death, rays funnel from afar
to my brown eye, to this ache of finger-rill stretch

stub toward pill bug who rolls in response, laughter
sings,

        sing to blackbird to raven to eagle to robin

red cheeks dimple under water, under tears, cat lick,

dog pink tongue, clicks of paws on tiles.

Water:

spray this thin mud,
        wash away salt and sand and clay,

lavage

        thin acid
           eat this pain

nudge, invite, call to

spider, fly, earthworm, caterpillar to roar a hospital's

support of care:
hummmmmm, hummmmmmm
air filter unit
oxygen

janitor's tread
mop slurp,
night beeps, thrills,

laughing gas to stop   to stop   to stop   to   stop   to   stop

Witch Spring, Isolation Day Nine

Hex reflex: let's change the world through viral twirl.
Ghost planes crisscross wizard marks above our heads

empty timetable elegy holds the slots of the air.
From the silver moon, shut-down urbanscapes

show clear skies. Breathe, fellow citizens of the world,
aromatherapy perfume of rose blossoms. Let it all lie

fallow, concrete sow's tits barren of oily industrial
milk. Next week's tech conference cancels itself.

Go to the phone. I do not streak across three state
lines to have a freaky coffee date at the giant mermaid

mega-store. The cauldron cooks. My fridge shoots
takeouts' white flags. A tiffin steals through the door,

witches' helper in stainless steel. Transport vehicles
hover clean, disinfected within an inch of their plastic

lives. The gig economy thrives in delivery stakes,
even if Uber burns, Shipt tips into the limelight.

Leave the bags in the pentagram on the curb,
do not cross the threshold. Deduct a trip a week,

five miles gained in an abacus of parsimony.
Netflix stock soars on prayer and thoughts.

The creeper roots you to the spot. Above,
reaper scythes contrails, we find old ruts,

our wagons skip like bears
    in the strangely warm forest air.

Skin Thirst

It is to be born.

Seventy days of brains leach viral eye juice crust.

Energy vortex revolts my limbic brain.

Quartered on the phone.

They arrived in waves of cut-off sound.

Such skin thirst sucks.

My ear crawls into the echo of delay,
    divided here   from then
        from them.

Loosen flexor rigor.

Drop the leg.

Your thesis stills somatic plants.

The disco:
    flaccid lumbar tango   angles my phone   hand closer to my hips
        grinds them an invite   into science fiction
        dream low gravity.

Those quartered ones, those shattered, reassemble on thin membranes.

Orchid frontal lobes applaud the tiniest drop of personal email magic.

I bear it, cleansed fingertips.

Membrane

Pour silent
    word honey onto

        deck's composite: grey resilient plastic

    water I remember dive

      iris's velvet tongue
        bumble's sticky black butt

      tender hairs.

Regurgitate: flower nectar pools in moon syrup

      soothe trachea

knit the wounds
    I remember a pollen grain
      school microscope ratchets up and down

This planet's sweet acid fills valleys
      between pink spiky extrusions.

I fondle a frayed book cover
    octagonal moon fields ready to fracture
      gently angular bucky sphere

      shields an air pilot's pleasure dome
calves exposed in Floridian swamp
mosquito whine

peer at horizon fire
lift-off to the stars
liquid force exhales the vacuum.

A breath—

Sticky lung sap captures sphere
cocaine holes

remember the cough

mucoidal flooding clears debris fields

red ball's spikes hook into logjam

beaver teeth fret at bloody molecules

I make my will in my mind

fruit-shaken

fever rubs my eyeballs raw.

Welcome to Your Viral Home

Spider heart, fill your body with hemolymph, pump it.

You don't know how to get there.
Hook your fingertips under the bone.

Push into sinus spaces   surround your silk glands.
            Dear spider,   fill your book lung
                        assemble hollow flat plates.

You don't. Smooth liver membrane.

            Circulate air in the library.
Spider heart, let hemolymph
        flow among the book plates.

Palpate your rib cage's edges.
Softness when you exhale.

        It's me.
The tight shark angles in from below.

            Book lung,   exchange carbon.
Here are the spiracles:
        open to the outside window.

Psoas intensity.
Lost on the streets, stitch in my side.

Use your   pedipalps
                        capture prey from the street
break it into very small fragments.

Floating ribs trail into pelvic matter.

There's a hook, and a rip.

Use your walking legs

Stand by the door.
to mince prey.

No, no, pain and me.
All is calm on the sea.
Your friends   will come.

Dear White Pine in My Garden

upon drifting in my backyard in Ypsilanti, Michigan

Thank you for the delicious syrup.

Your five-bundled fascicles cleave the alveoli of my lungs.

Lances stir mucus, leave vitamin C in the brew.

At the farthest ends of my arterial capillaries, slick whiff of aroma lenses a molecule through the membrane's barn door.

You lodge, a mini tree, in DNA passed down through my maternal line, farm women with hands in faraway soil where what was wrapped in muslin, sunk into tea kettle and boiled all day between Napoleon's soldiers, long treks to silk factories, hoot of titanic engines on briny seas, mirrored itself in a New Country, there grew wild and tall.

We gather you now, new flu with old expectorants, ballast for the graveyards of our living rooms.

Galleons come to a standstill, oak timber decays into ribs on our beaches.

Dear pine, your soft wood smoothed the midship's deck, salted and sugared.

You dissolved first, fibers rent by sea birds.

Leached-out needles make for compost row.

Acidic, you bite the land back, long for the sea, channel stuckness into flow.

Protect us, dear pine, let me root here, back bowed, hands flat.

Travel Edges: Lunch time, Costanoa, Cascade Café, Pacific Coast, California

upon drifting along California's coast

Logs, notched for the ceiling beams. Braced, steel manacle, sleeve. Traditional lodge design in camping ground. Ricotta pancakes, savory, full of bacon bits. Scrambled eggs and sourdough bread, toasted with a touch of flame. An old photograph, framed by a thin black funereal stripe. Big Tree Grove, Santa Cruz. A white logger lies in the scar of a giant tree, a redwood, primed to fall away from him in just a few dangerous strokes of the axe he holds vertical:

> the axe, upright, after having compromised the uprightness of the tree, the gap vaginal, ex-virginal, to be claimed by his beard, his garters, the denim shirt. A day's work well done, repose, with a wink to the jubilatory daguerreotype visitor, admiring the brawny yet lean muscles. Next to the logger's left arm, alone in the tree shadow,   his hat, soft and molded, textures of calf skin, velvet, creeping away to where still alive heartwood cells touch brethren, breathe with one liquid stroke up and down the giant stem.

Desert Song

upon drifting in Joshua Tree National Park

Lizards slither, at least, their skin might not stick so much. Mine sticks, desert crystals roughing up the smoothness of river stone. This water was too long ago, eon ocean

battered rounds that smell of water, perfume, coy, a veil of water draped so long ago. Gone. All done and drained. Spirited away on desert fumes, heat death.

Crystals grow, accrete, erode, I imagine fractals in the tiny spires under my tender palm. Careful now, do not scratch retina, shoe leather, twist that ankle lest dinosaur

bones grow out of your desiccated flesh. Half-full water bottle glides unanchored down rounded hump of super whale, out of reach in the sand nest, verbena viper lair, the scorpion's climate sting shivers in spring rain mirage, desert blooms, one day, another, hipster coffee bar and bathhouse stink erased in mud

prints, hoof print, lizards pad softly, softly, down the curve, Earth's own curve, this tiny mudball, sandstone's ancient uncle, ur-sea.

Ammonite curled deep inside itself,
tentacles twisted inward, waiting,

waiting,

for the ocean to swell once more.

Isolation/Skinner Releasing

Spider sticks up
knee impetus,

elbow softens
into query:

clock ticking, rain drops.
Smell of pressed wood panels

skull strings just above my ears:

Portal opens:
synth riffs up doors to stars
archives of bubbles
trail exhortation

Uneven floor city grime beneath naked toes.
Hip sockets run loose   melt into the wooden grain.

Deep drums yank into mammoth rhythm.
Fat runs in billows over the first floor,
harmonics race in midsummer arches.

Light floods

arc of flax tension jolts up
golden lines to universe.

My eyes fly over exercise yard.
I step into the installation
no one's puppet but my own.

Blood pounds, upward vocal reach,
circular plates drench me in color.
                    Hips flange out: moth wings.

Red vestibule, stained glass
string winds around Mars, tugs up.
Bones melt into wax

          dark cathedral light

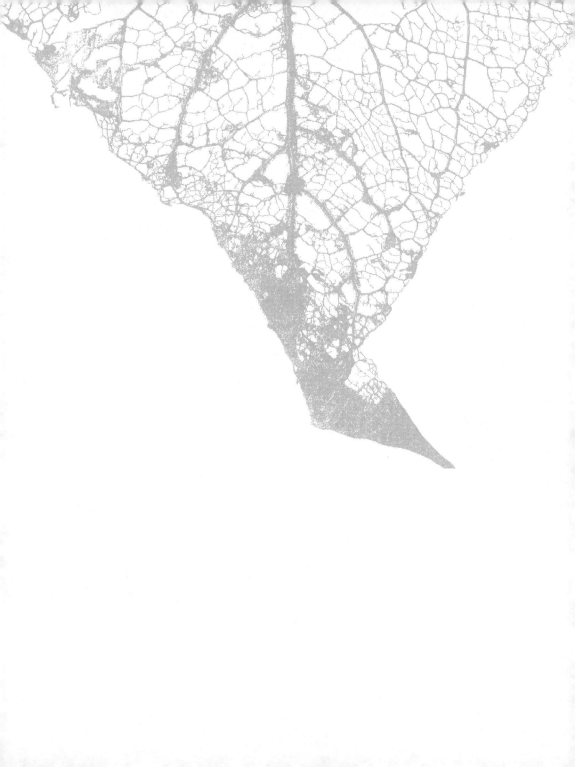

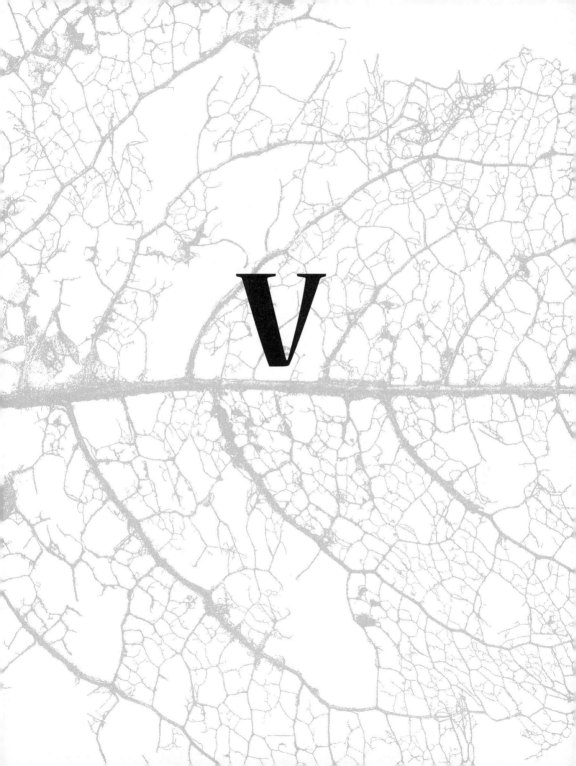

V

Book Lungs

Paint over creases in the paper, in the archive, swish that color right into the edges till we shine, you and I, we shine, bodies submerged emerge in the beaten still-white page, skirt watery dispersion to assemble, molecule by molecule, toward a reach, a breach, a stretch that lifts the chasm out of my life.

Paint in thick pastes to spackle over the cracks.

Each squeeze displaces vacuum.

Tiny spider finds a new home as the thickness rolls, licks, and blobs.

The hollow bursts into contour, texture, with each breath and slap, it swells and hardens into new land, fit for a tender foot or tendril.

And then there are hills and plains and the plants I knew by the ditch's side, and the weight of the kohlrabi head in my hand, and the feel of the rusty-dusty grid shielding the Station of the Cross out there, in the middle of the field, and there was the witch's leaky gondola, in an ancient castle never found again, the thicket that never appears again, a mirage on the field grounds, flat horizon falters against my sense memory.

Pain thins, paint thickens, a wash of memory glistens on the land.

Unsettled: the sediment stirs into a new pattern.

Mix it, pigment it, rub charcoal from ancient trees burned cinder hard a long time ago.

You and I, we build a fire, red orange blossoms out of old receipts, contracts, out-of-date maps.

We trace new districts in rising heat, each arc caresses bioluminescent motes that enliven the air of our accreting, shielding, living lungs.

We live as archives in the world, you and I, our book lungs spidering the land with ghost marks, a tramp's alphabet to signal: paint this nest.

Here you can rest.

Moon Map in My Ypsilanti Backyard, in the Afternoon Thunderstorm

Mare oculus, collect the light that falls as prism
color code micro-smells in the rain.
Mare os, guide me down into dark caverns
wet moss beneath my feet.
Mare nasus, to the weaving interior fields of stalks, reach
leather green of pine needles, black twigs.
Mare finditur, rift opens below the nose's saddle
too tiny for my fingertips.
Mare mentum, a final hill, drip
rivulets, slide side of my neck.
Wet shoulders, cool, explode green fire, eye falls blur
liquid curtain waves, glass raindrops sing color transition.
Rhythms: cloud rain, tree rain,
tattoos my backspace, moistens my spine.

The Bread

> But was it ever small like that, the first body?
> Did it ever sit close to the ants and their piles
> of dirt from which that body had come?
> —Camille Dungy, "From the First, the Body Was Dirt"

The bread. Smell the moist hunk of it, abandoned by the side of the street near the chiropractor's door, just step toward it, over to the apple tree. Fermentation is in the air, look close and see worm-wriggle just beneath cheek blush. The bread swells out, pores open, breath-full. The bag has burst wetly, white holes and grains spill like dandelion fluff from plastic webs. Cider-sour mold stains squashed grass.

Follow decay juice down, gravity pulls, to the strata of tiny springtails, hexapod microorganisms, which each squish a chip of white-green mold bread compound down to their caverns, through cave tunnels between loose crumbles of soil. Make friends: wave at her compound eye, see yourself reflected in the last dying light— there you are, so many times, as she munches her treasure in peace.

A giant earthworm moves by you two, majestic and pink, this corer leaves a round hole for springtail and you to follow. Earth grows dark. Springtail nods at family deep below: colorless carapace Auntie, long having abandoned surface ways. Auntie's sisters make a wreath in the round cave, a portal: Will you step through? That fluff of ever greener bread you drag slithers across antennae, translucent torsos where pale hemolymph pumps through the dorsal vessel's thickening pipe.

Beyond the portal: a cathedral opens, phosphorous lights on beetles' backends reveal a cavern. You scan a ribbed vault, earth packed tight as moist clay between bony stays. A rumble ahead. You follow the sound wave with your devolving eyes, your midline pings out in response. Ears travel inward. Your feet are gone.

Deep in the cavern, a skitter, crackle, thump-thump base note: ground beetles, wings long atrophied, scratch against one another in a round heap, a horde hundred bodies deep and more, constant motion, mandibles out and rasping. The ball resonates against the overhead arcs of ribs. The vault that once housed lungs massages this mass now, motion/sound vibrations, a roar in the earth.

Transformation. You approach this beat, this push, with your disaggregate of wilted moldy bread, drips of vinegary moisture mark the brown earth pack where you crawl, until the ball rears right here: beetle sharpness of waxy chitin, armor, wave at you as they plow under, over, never tire. Jaws that reach deep into the coil of a snail extract a last cling of flesh, leave behind a tiny porcelain jewel between giant vertebrae cemented into the ground.

Forty antennae, then ninety mandibles, then too many razor legs reach forward, toward you, toward your hand, your tentacle, that sensitive pad, pluck the fuzzy weeping bread mold offering. Metallic clicks mesmerize, then tick over you, the carrier, pluck and pull. You see large beetle eyes close, so close. Antennae caress every micrometer, invite, breathe, recycle, compost, each breath, each breath, till you are inside. Embrace.

Ghost Bridge of Ford Lake

> No one has driven over the bridge in years, but it is still there on the flats. . . .
> There, on the bottom of Ford Lake, is where it rests today.
>
> —James Mann, local historian, *MLive*

At night, the Ford Lake Dam still hums.

Old Hydro buzzes in his sleep, jumps shivers down deformed bullhead catfish spines.

Deep beneath, the Sauk Indian Trail remembers soles that anchored river to the land—*tramp, climb, traverse*—footprints chime from fort to village, trade post, friend.

Cyanobacteria now whisper the messages in blue-green sibilants: *spill, spill, this made thing, earth dam, iron suspension, tremble on the land. We will we will we will run away and rush and cleanse and sweep away sandstone, metal shavings, Fordite scraps of car color lacquered in layers, this palimpsest of racy longings, ram shiny fins in baby blue and rose that parade on Sunday down Depot Town.*

The factory presses rectangles onto the rusty earth.

Ant workers crawl into chocolate cake segments layered next to the lake.

Air intake valves pierce the rain sky.

Tonight, close by, the Ypsilanti Ford Motor Plant lassos a sinus wave of power: *kick the starters, traverse voltage regulators, jump ignition coils.*

All tune—fish, soil, iron, tiny algae—till brake cylinders caress and channel all energy to the tomb.

Earth Séance

> what blows/ in curbside weeds is not insect embroidery, deal/ with us. We are
> the dead.
>
> —Justin Phillip Reed, "If We Must Be the Dead"

Quartered, you enter.   Vivisected, you enter.
          Push   toward   dispersal
scatter yourself   to the water   winds.
          Slime sensation   drains through   soil,
mix with   compost   and mulch:
          metal core,   magnetic,   pulse.
Worm mouths,   cool and soft,   slide along edges,
sunshine   warms through   the inches,
                    sucks moisture upward.
Release   hormones,   pheromones,
          scent molecule to drift:
drift over
          drift toward   the river
                                      drift toward   Lake Erie.
Sun   wind   ice   slides   all year
          all year   you lose   yourself to   multitudes.
Fragment   filaments   entangle   with sticky
water   with carbon   dusted snow.
          PFAS   eternal elements   cling to   mercurial
tension drop,   elongate,   do not let go, clasp
so hard   to this spot,   slot in the bone
in the fatty   tissue of the drop   of the eyelid.
In the earth séance,   you are drawn to it all,
          to the veils   of the sky   and the deep brown dark
Earth   core   and the shimmering root.
          You slide   along the channels   of this soil,
microbial   dance,   chemical scepter,
ballroom   of this square inch   holds you in thrall.

Turtle Disco

upon performing as part of Full Pink Moon, Opera Povera in Quarantine: *a durational livestream performance of composer Pauline Oliveros, April 7, 2020*

She shimmers silver

suburban room glows like an ice rink

she crawls through the microphone

there's a green glow around my liver

immune support on the gong

alone in the night sky, a dream

purple beads drip from here to Chicago

her Full Pink Moon tutu crown

flicks across my lips

grease paint dissolves into almond cream

no note is wrong in the universal hum

three hours in, midnight is a slow river

my shoulders press the steel-tongue drum

fingers vibrate, cool metal cry

hypnogogic caress of darkness

She rises high

Starship over Eastern Michigan University

upon drifting on Eastern Michigan University's campus, integrating snippets
from historical documents, maps, and photos

The university pulls her in.

Overhead, clouds rip apart.

She walks, kicks a raccoon's
  turd to the curb.

Brown streaks on asphalt.

The cafeteria sprawls lewd in the sunshine.

Metal cylinder pushes through.

Her thighs piston.

Her polka-dotted mini skirt rucks
   up, she drags it
     down.

     Sunspot lenses up,
   ratchets into focus
as she bends.

Pink pleather belt squishes air out of her belly.

An earring in her hand.

She runs.

   Eyes target her path.

Smoke curls up from fire-spots.

Asphalt softens into ice cream.

She angles up her knees
        like a crane.
                Eyeliner smokes
        into pink eye.

Above, they squeal,
        finger
                the control panel.

        Doors grin welcome.

She sprints into the library.

Tree Futures

Weep viscous tears to smear across
this small tin and fretwork starship,

my garden's new delight. Dear pine,
arms stretched to breaking point

in ballet pose, cradle this new star
shot hope, weep to smother hair-cracks

with resin. Just yesterday, a mosquito
tree-touched for a suck. The pierced

pale bubble welled up, grabbed foot hook,
launched over swollen abdomen,

tiny wings, stilled to petrify the flight.
Dear pine, lay down your rotten bones.

I cleave them with this murder axe,

launch into skies

      a sacrifice

            to burn so bright

                against the crescent moon.

Split/Screen

July energies in the air float like an oily zeppelin
around around around with no friction but time

hubcap swirls like a broken deer upside down on the street
red and blue and white and night and the wheel, the wheel

pause slides in the warmth, drop-down a weird January air
passage opens between my ribs as I probe into

car crash wheels hum above glass crystals surround
blood and glass light and blood light and glass and red-blue light
and sirens and hands and blood and a belt and a cut and hands
and fall gently and cheek on glass that is not sharp but blood
blood drop in my lashes blink red and blue light white moon snow
glass in the dark in the red in the blood in the skin in the scar

Summer wheels spin. Bang. Howling lights outside, vibrate glass.
Read the Detroit report in the café, a drop of absinthe swirls water

veils. Beat. Outside, the rain. Coffee smells mingle with fried onions.
Hip bones sink and anchor on wood. Light rhythms paint the window.

My gullet is empty, endless, a void slick with ground glass festers
into pain, pulls me into time river, moonlight sucks down to snow.

Gothic

upon drifting at Lillie Park, Ann Arbor

Poison sumac: red gothic earrings on gnarled fingerbones.

Velvet touch of a lamb's ears cabbage patch, linden-green pulse in the ground.

Black garbage bags, burnt into devil finger's fungus.

Rake up a blue shirt. Orange netting lichen.

A shaped metal thing, as if a locomotive brayed it toward spread.

Bitumen patches, rain-curled out of seals.

Dinosaur seed pods, swollen purple with green sticky sap.

Acorn nut, un-hatted, veined, split, keeps the secret.

Eventide

I grasp the sit-on lawn mower's wheel
      ripple this land,
        hillocks bump under blade
nearby road's car tire
          rubber dust dots
dark green space
        beneath grass hair
wind-smooth blade
      falls into decay.
How far down does light penetrate?
       Energy gifts ping off,
          fractal toward brown,
            toward invasion,
        maceration bubble gas
luminescent at night,
         green bone child,
       rain drives nutrients into flow,
        course
down the culvert,
       rapture cuttings to edge
       where they hang,
        hold on,
          precarious balance,
sodden mass deposit
       leaches
         juice toward
       cascading river's sluice,
Lake Erie's smooth mouth
       sips bone broth,
         spears align along
       the compass to the shed

trickle slow,
    earth child,
        race with the storm

       to rivering
       to open

              to dissolve

The Princess, the Frog, and Iron Heinrich

Based on a famous Brothers Grimm Märchen, likely part of the oral tradition of the family Wild in Kassel. Wilhelm Grimm eventually married Dortchen Wild against her father's wishes.

The princess just wanted to play.
The princess enjoyed her round golden ball.
The princess breathed in the forest.
The princess bathed her feet in the well.

Why did gravity not obey her wishes?
Why did the ball go awry?

Why wasn't she allowed to swim, naked and glorious, into the dark water, the deep well, the spring in the forest, to roll and glide like the wild thing she was?

She had to ask the frog, of course.

And the frog was not wild. The frog sat by the evening lamp at the kitchen table in Kassel, visiting with the family Wild. Far away, the frog's servant, Iron Heinrich, bled rust from his heart's iron belts onto the castle's grey bleak slate.

Mrs. Wild stabbed her embroidery, once, twice, thrice, till something bled: her thumb, or maybe the ancestral line.

Dortchen Wild shared a bit of cake from her porcelain plate with starving Wilhelm Grimm. She looked down at her ethnographic notes. All the fairy tales.

The frog cleared his throat. I want to lie in your comfy bed, upstairs, downstairs, down the well, in the cellar with the washing machine.

In the kitchen the princess shuddered and made a new mark. Father Wild barked. Mrs. Wild stabbed herself through the cloth, deep into her thigh.

The princess wanted just a bit of it, just a dip, let it rip in the late afternoon sun, fronds of ferns over her breasts, the silken milk of her German skin, fingers wet and all the open open open open.

The frog didn't like his spots, his moss green livery, the feel of flies in his teeth. Frog said:

Throw me against the wall, princess, hard as you can, just use these raw red fists.

I laugh and I am the motorcycle man, the candy-colored clown they call the sandman.

The prince and the father and their witness, Iron Heinrich, went for a manly walk in the dark. There were shots, three bands of iron broke loose, and the geese flew high so high so far.

Beneath the table, Dortchen scrubbed and scrubbed at the bloodied carpet, hair wild, heart drum, fingers full of pain, and the blood and ink married each other and ran down the drain.

That's where the iron floods, the deep vein in the well of the forest.

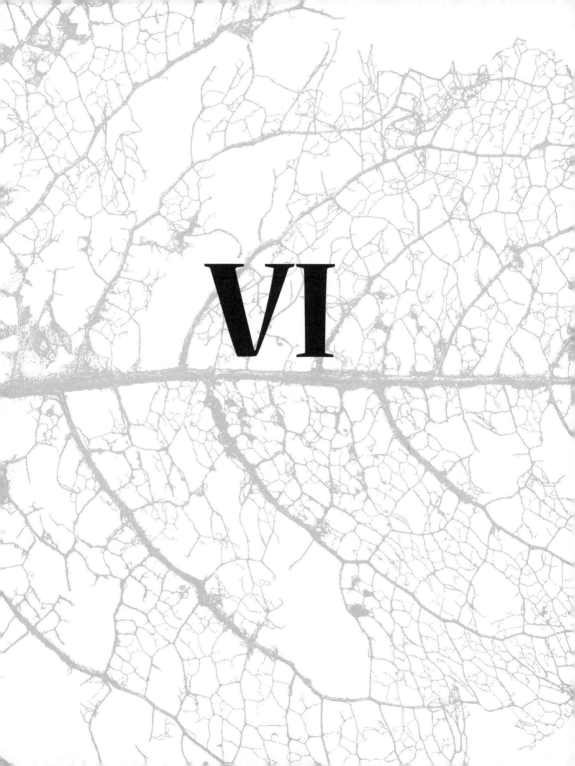

VI

The Diver Revisited

The diver faces the monster.

The monster tastes the bitter water.

The bitter water bathes the other monster.

Everybody dances in the draft, toe reach, tired.

It is hot.

It is cold.

Disoriented monster.

Vent smells of Bacardi cola.

The diver lets out globes of air.

They sail up,
       silver,
          glossy,
                 toward surface.

The surface burps back,   impact radiant deep and turpentine,
        brown swirls shred into   heavy blue.

The first monster hits the diver.

The second monster throws a monster foot
       onto the silicon creature,   heat-soaked,
     purple with grey lips that mouth
       the diver's leg,   precious hose,
rams into the mud,

                        breaks into atoms,
            skinsack tight,
                        caress,   a living wriggle
            signals to   the monster.

Flash.

Turn.

Horny scales pinch rubber.

The second monster glides close.

Tongue rasps scales open.

Hormones knit calcium,   birth
            corpuscles in the salt,   brine,
                        amoeba
            tango in anaerobic curves.

The diver sucks,
            pulses,
                        ventral mouth
            belly anus,   massages nervous system
                        to radial spread.

Play ring, squish

            pressure.

Turn the legs in, pelvis release.

The diver somersaults,   arrows up,
                        surface high above lances nourishment,
            diver finds arms, finds ear,
                        seashell blood all lymph,   all jelly.

The monsters watch,   cat's cradle between
umami seaweed tangles   toward flow.

Diver coruscates.

Above, so far, surface
        conceals.

        Monsters One and Two

        blow a new world.

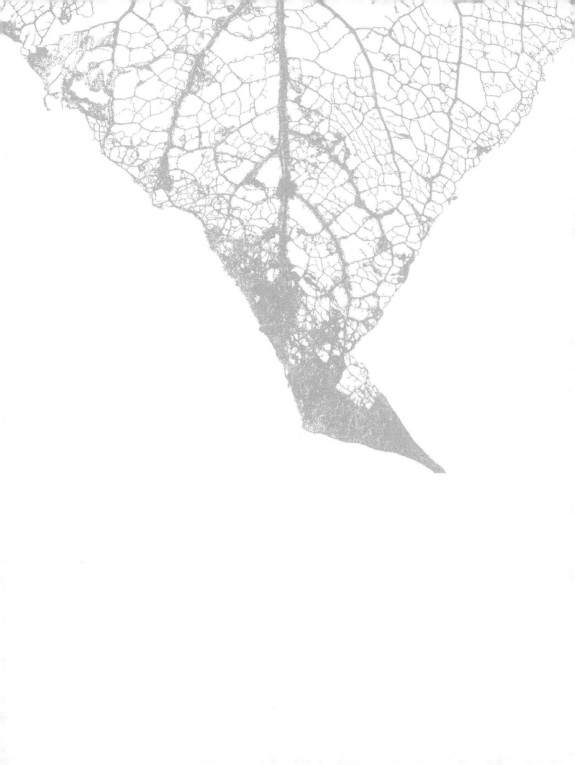

Notes

The Huron River, an important trade route for thousands of years, carries a colonial name that references Indigenous people. Incoming French traders called the Wyandot "Hurons," a reference to bristle-hair, also an insult along the lines of "ruffian." The Wyandot named the river Giwitatigweiasibi, or "burnt-oak region," likely a reference to Indigenous fire control practices.

Indigenous and settler entwinements in the region are numerous. Before forced removal in 1840, a principal Potawatomi village stood on the banks of the river in what is now colonially known as Ypsilanti. Manipulated treaties between Governor Lewis Cass, after whom an area of Detroit is named, and the Anishinaabeg provided land for the University of Michigan.

Many industries have released toxins into the river, including per- and polyfluoroalkyl substances (PFAS), forever chemicals, which now threaten the local water supply.

"Compass": I am swimming with Adrienne Rich's "Diving into the Wreck" throughout the book.

"Dancing Princesses": This poem is based on a fairy tale collected by the Brothers Grimm, with Jenny von Droste-Hülshoff as one of their female informants, intersected with material about the Ypsilanti and Detroit Murders.

"Reintegration": Hair clippings and black paint in a basement a few doors down from my home were part of the clues that led to the Michigan Murderer's arrest.

Earthworms appear in multiple poems in this collection. They are European settlers who came with the colonizers in the 1600s, arriving in root balls and ballast. Earlier worms probably existed in the northern woods but had been wiped out by the ice sheets of the last glaciation. Some memories are soft-bodied and do not appear in the fossil records.

"Michigan Murders": I harvested lines from the 1969–1970 press coverage of the Ypsilanti Murders. Other references from regional history appear as well, like the Detroit Algiers Motel's racially motivated police murders in 1967.

"Orderly Street Ghost": Building in the floodplain of the Huron River creates many problems in climate change times. In 2021, part of my neighborhood flooded to the level of FEMA disaster assistance. Stephanie Heit created a rain garden for our home, calculated to dissipate runoff, hold against erosion, and detoxify, one of the many small mitigation efforts underway at the individual and municipal level. This poem and others reference plants in our rain garden.

"Foundation Ore": One of the murdered women of Ypsilanti was found near a street culvert as workers were preparing the ground for a new housing development. In recent decades, many abandoned homes in Detroit were stripped of copper, lead, and other metal. Much of Michigan's infrastructure is old, and civic neglect allows lead to escape into water and air.

"Tunnels": These three interwoven strands emerged in an Amoeba Dance session I led in Turtle Disco, the somatic writing studio I co-create with Stephanie Heit in our home in Ypsilanti. In group sessions, we use sounds to tunnel through our bodies, listen to the echoes and waves that travel through us, and eventually distill these signals into writing.

Martín Ramírez was a Mexican artist who was incarcerated in Californian mental hospitals. In my sessions, we honor his artwork, woven into this poem, and honor him as a lineage holder and elder.

"Welcome to Your Viral Home": This and other poems remediate anatomy information about spiders, co-inhabitants of my domestic sphere, in the edge spaces of Turtle Disco.

"Dear White Pine in My Garden": This is an ode to a particular pine tree, one that supported me during my first encounter with COVID-19. My friend and herbalist Beth Currans made a tincture from this pine's needles, and I drank this to help me regain lung function.

"Isolation/Skinner Releasing": This is a form of somatic movement work, based on Joan Skinner's technique that combines image-guided movements with anatomical alignment.

"Moon Map in My Ypsilanti Backyard": A mare is a flat, dark plain of lower elevation on the moon, observable through telescopes. The term means "sea" in Latin, and I am using other Latin terms for facial parts to create my own embodied celestial map.

"Split/Screen": This poem metabolizes what happened to me during a choir tour in northern Germany when our car careened in icy conditions. My fellow choristers and I survived, one with a broken neck. I had a near-death experience, which wiped out more than a year's worth of memories. Parts of my university life before this travel accident are still hazy to me.

Gratitude

Poetry is a communal endeavor, a witnessing of movement through time and space, in human and more-than-human company.

Thanks to the land, and to the many nourishing retreat times I experience in the region I call home, as a white settler on Ojibwe, Odawa, Potawatomi, and Wyandot territories, in Ypsilanti (Ypsi), Michigan. I honor the elders past, present, and future who steward these lands.

Thanks also to Wildacres Retreat, North Carolina; Writers' Colony at Dairy Hollow artist residency, Eureka, Arkansas; Good Hart Artist Residency, Michigan; Surel's Place Artist Residency, Boise, Idaho; and many visits and conversations with my fellow fellows at the Black Earth Institute, Wisconsin.

Both local and faraway residencies offered me space to develop this collection, to sit with death and violence unequally distributed, to question my ethics, to shake as I probed the connections to my own personal fears, to death fantasies, to the lure of horror. Many rural residencies offered me the other side of this collection's perspective: soil, geology, botanical encounters and zoological inspirations, the creeping slithering teeming glorious life of breakdown and recycling.

As a disabled woman, I often sit close to the ground, at rest while others hike. I sat and watched the drama unfold beneath the decaying leaves, or I used ink and watercolor to hold on to the elemental processes I witnessed. I thank the Washtenaw Community College Urban Sketching group for companionship on some of these journeys.

True crime narratives, listening, and space were deeply intwined for me when I first delved into the genre through travel reading and audiobooks. I thank the Ann Arbor Public Library: I found Edward M. Keyes's 1976 *Michigan Murders* there while on the way to the Detroit airport. I remember the fabric texture of the library chair where I first read Maggie Nelson's *Jane: A Murder*. I also remember being in the grip of Truman Capote's *In Cold Blood* while driving through the dark forests of Northern California, on my way to Orr Hot Springs. One of my journeys from Ypsi to Up North Michigan vibrated in the aural space of Ann Rule's *Stranger Beside Me*, both genre and delivery intermixing with the fact that Rule worked at a suicide hotline with Ted Bundy. Much later, I listened to the first *Serial* podcast episodes while driving near Pigeon Point Lighthouse in Pescadero, California.

Much true crime fiction is focused on white cis women victims and crime protagonists. I am grateful for books like Bryan Stevenson's *Just Mercy*, Ron Stallworth's

Black Klansman, and Danez Smith's poetry collection *Don't Call Us Dead*, which offer Black-framed perspectives on a racist justice industrial complex. Likewise, few true crime books focus on the precarity and resilience of queer and trans lives, and I am grateful for the work of writers like Justin Ling and his *Missing from the Village*, and Kathryn Miles's *Trailed*.

My last two poetry collections were informed in part by media representations of femicides on the Mexico-U.S. border and anti-women violence in Indigenous/ settler contexts. I am grateful for the many authors writing on these topics, including Jessica McDiarmid and her *Highway of Tears*, with its focus on relationships and circles in narrating the lives of murdered Indigenous women, and Cynthia Pelayo and her poetry collection, *Into the Forest and All the Way Through*, which charts moments of many missing women's lives.

What to narrate, what to leave out, and the effects of racism, class privilege, and misogyny on public moral judgment—these issues are at stake in this collection, as you can easily find out if you start searching for details about the murders.

Human-on-human violence is the terrain of true crime, but my attention shifted again and again to the wider ecologies of violence: toxicities and the forever chemicals like PFAS that seeped like old ballast into the ground; the unequal distribution of precarity and opportunity in a racialized world and the brown fields left behind in the wake of land zoning; what counts as gardens, what counts as wilderness, and how the borders are policed. I thank the many activists who hold us accountable by presenting the evidence of unequal burdens, draw attention to toxic loads, and try to find solutions to move toward balance. In particular, I wish to thank the Environmental Humanities/Poetics group created by Angela Hume, and the rich discussion we had about our readings.

Many thanks to Eastern Michigan University, which awarded me the 2022–23 McAndless Distinguished Professor Chair, which allowed me to work and play with students and faculty on some of the themes of this collection. Special thanks to Beth Currans, Jim Egge, Carla Harryman, Decky Alexander, and, in particular, Christine Hume, whose ongoing work on anti-women violence in Ypsi has influenced my approaches.

Thanks to the helpful librarians of the Map Library at the University of Michigan, who pulled out many regional maps of my neighborhood, spanning over a century. Thanks also to my wonderful neighbors in College Heights, our Ypsilanti neighborhood, who shared their memories with me, and to local historian Matthew Siegfried and his neighborhood walks.

This book emerged when many of these themes played out bodily for all humans in the lockdown period of the ongoing COVID-19 crisis, amid the many questions the pandemic raised. Whose bodymindspirits were marked for disposability? Where do the corpses land? How does the land respond to changed human movement patterns? How does it feel to witness the scarring violence in my own lungs? I thank the disabled activists who quickly responded to the crisis and modeled mutual support, such as the late Stacey Milbern and the Disability Justice Culture Club in the Bay Area. I thank the many nurses and others working within a broken medical system.

COVID-19 art collectives were so central to my experience of the lockdown and my own healing from COVID-19. I thank Laura Kasischke for her daily poetry prompt community in March/April 2020; the Belladonna* Collaborative for their synchronous walks and Zooms; my weekly creative engagements with Vidhu Aggarwal and DJ Lee; my plant horror exploration with Megan Kaminski; and my writing times with Denise Leto. I also cherish the first weekly, now monthly, kaffeeklatsches of our Turtle Disco disability culture collective. Thanks also to the poet/scientists of our monthly ecopoetry collective, Mary Newell, Jennifer Spector, Rebecca Durham, Laurie Anderson, and more.

I thank the many participants of the EcoSomatics symposium series (2018–2021), in particular, the *Eco Monsters and Somatic Takeovers* events held in various gardens in Ypsilanti, outdoors, in September 2021. Dancers, somatic movement artists, and writers came together to explore monstrous shapes as ancestors, as present bodymindspirits, and as speculative embodiments, conceived in viral times. My thanks to Marc Arthur, Biba Bell, Charli Brissey, Stefanie K. Dunning, Cara Hagen, Christina Vega-Westhoff, Kathy Westwater, moira williams, and Stephanie Heit. Also many thanks to the Speculative Embodiment Working Group at the University of Michigan, who continued exploring these queries with me.

So many Zoom experiments in movement/writing supported my work, including the Open Source Forms Summer Intensive 2022 with Stephanie Skura; MELT workshops with the TRY team of Ishmael Houston-Jones, Keith Hennessy, Snowflake Calvert, jose e. abad, and Kevin O'Connor; and Skinner Releasing work with Yvonne Meier and Julie Mayo.

The core support that makes my work possible is the creative compost of Turtle Disco, the queer/disabled local somatic writing community Stephanie Heit and I lead out of our living room in Ypsilanti, Michigan. When the pandemic first hit, we moved our offerings into the Zoomshell. Many thanks in particular to all Turtle Disco regulars and to the contributors to the *Pandemic Artifacts // From the Zoomshell* chapbook: Elena SV Flys, Chanika Svetvilas, Victoria Lee Khatoon, Naomi Ortiz, Jose Miguel Esteban, Tracy Veck, Denise Leto, Marc Arthur, Samar Abulhassan, Roxanna Bennett, Raven

Kame'enui-Becker, Beth Currans, Sarah Dean, Megan Kaminski, and Hannah Soyer.

Thank you, fabulous readers of this collection in its various stages: Megan Kaminski, Vidhu Aggarwal, Denise Leto, Renee Wehrle, and Stephanie Heit. I thank you deeply for your insights and encouragement.

Wayne State University Press has been a delight to work with again: so many thanks to the whole team!

And, again and again, thank you, my love, my collaborator, my creative partner and wife, the dancer, poet, diver, Stephanie Heit.

Acknowledgments

"Dancing Princesses": *Frog Island Chapbook*

"Reintegration": *Denver Quarterly*

"Fungi Moves," "Night Crawler," and "Tree Futures": *The Goose: Moving on Land*

"Coventry Street, Detroit": *Zócalo Public Square*

"Foundation Ore" and "Welcome to Your Viral Home," as part of Zoom Somatics in
   Four Poems (mini essay and four poems): *Edge Effects*

"Tunnels": *Venti Journal*

"Witch Spring" and "Dear Pine": *Poetics for the More-than-Human World: An Anthology
   of Poetry and Commentary*

"Skin Thirst": *Hello Goodbye Apocalypse*

"Membrane": *About Place: When We Are Lost/How We Are Found*

"Travel Edges: Lunch time, Costanoa, Cascade Café, Pacific Coast, California":
   About Place: Infinite Country

"Desert Song": *About Place: Works of Resistance and Resilience*

"Skinner Releasing": *(home)Body*, an art installation by Cid Pearlman Performance

"Book Lungs": *Orion Magazine*

"Moon Map in my Ypsilanti Backyard, in the Afternoon Thunderstorm": *Ploughshares*

"Ghost Bridge": *About Place: Center of Gravity*

"Earth Séance": *Zoeglossia*, part of the Poetry Coalition's on grief programming

"Turtle Disco" and "The Diver": *Sinister Wisdom*

"Split/Screen": *Texas Review*

"Gothic": *Plumwood Mountain Journal: An Australian and International Journal of
   Ecopoetry & Ecopoetics*

"Eventide": *Plants and Poetry Journal: Wildlife of the Underworld*

Lines of various poems have appeared in encaustic paintings and drawings exhibited in
the region.

Bibliography

Bryant Logan, William. *Dirt: The Ecstatic Skin of the Earth*. W. W. Norton, 1995.

Capote, Truman. *In Cold Blood*. Random House, 1966.

de la Perrière, Donna. *Works of Love & Terror*. Talisman House, 2019.

Doris, Stacy. *Knot*. Georgia University Press, 2006.

Dungy, Camille. "From the First, the Body Was Dirt." *Poetry*, December 2011.

Elfrink, Tim. "'I'm about to die': A woman escaped a serial killer by stabbing him and jumping out a window, police say." *Washington Post*, September 6, 2019.

Heit, Stephanie, and Petra Kuppers, eds. *Pandemic Artifacts // From the Zoomshell*. Turtle Disco Press, 2021.

Hume, Christine. *Everything I Never Wanted to Know*. The Ohio State University Press, 2023.

Hunter, George. "Possible serial murders shine light on Detroit's vacant homes," *The Detroit News*, June 7, 2019.

Keyes, Edward M. *Michigan Murders*. Pocket Books, 1976.

Koenig, Sarah. *Serial: Season One*. Produced by Sarah Koenig, Julie Snyder, Dana Chivvis, and Emily Condon. This American Life, 2014.

Ling, Justin. *Missing from the Village: The Story of Serial Killer Bruce McArthur, the Search for Justice, and the System That Failed Toronto's Queer Community*. Penguin, 2020.

Mann, James. "An old bridge rests under water instead on top of it," *MLive*, July 27, 2008.

McDiarmid, Jessica. *Highway of Tears: A True Story of Racism, Indifference, and the Pursuit of Justice for Missing and Murdered Indigenous Women and Girls*. Penguin, 2020.

Miles, Kathryn. *Trailed: One Woman's Quest to Solve the Shenandoah Murders*. Algonquin, 2022.

Nelson, Maggie. *Jane: A Murder*. Soft Skull, 2005.

Pelayo, Cynthia. *Into the Forest and All the Way Through*. Burial Day Books, 2020.

Reed, Justin Phillip. *The Malevolent Volume*. Coffee House Press, 2020.

Rich, Adrienne. *Diving into the Wreck: Poems 1971–1972*. W. W. Norton, 1973.

Rule, Ann. *Stranger Beside Me*. W. W. Norton, 1980.

Salcedo, Angelina. "'We've never seen this before': Pulmonologists say lung scans show devastating impacts from COVID-19." *WTSP 10 Tampa Bay*. February 19, 2021.

Smith, Danez. *Don't Call Us Dead*. Graywolf, 2017.

Stallworth, Ron. *Black Klansman: Race, Hate, and the Undercover Investigation of a Lifetime*. Blackiron Books, 2018.

Stevenson, Bryan. *Just Mercy: A Story of Justice and Redemption*. Spiegel and Grau, 2014.

Wolcheck, Rob. "Michigan Murders: 50 years ago, terror in Ypsilanti ends." *FOX 2 Detroit*, July 26, 2019.

"Woman found murdered in rolled up carpet at abandoned home on east side." *FOX 2 Detroit*, June 13, 2019.

About the Author

Petra Kuppers is a disability culture activist and a community performance artist who uses somatics, performance, and speculative writing to engage audiences toward more socially just and enjoyable futures. She is the Anita Gonzalez Collegiate Professor of Performance Studies and Disability Culture at the University of Michigan, a 2023 Guggenheim Fellow, and codirector of the somatic writing studio Turtle Disco.

Tamara Wade

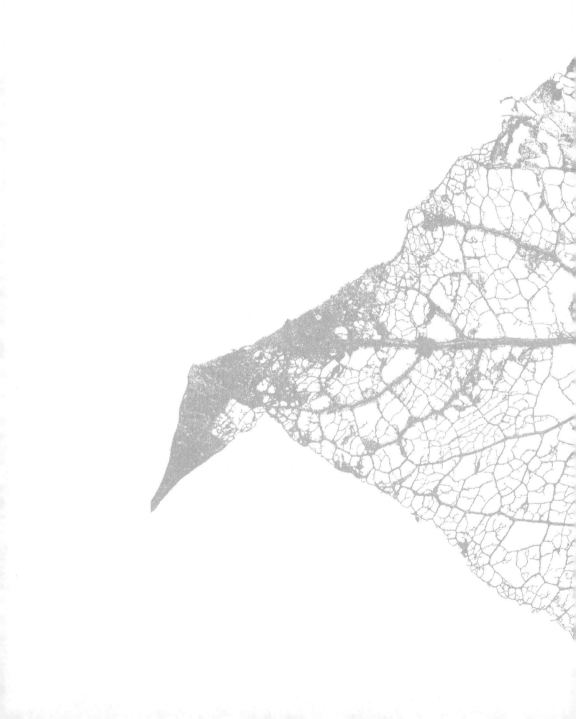

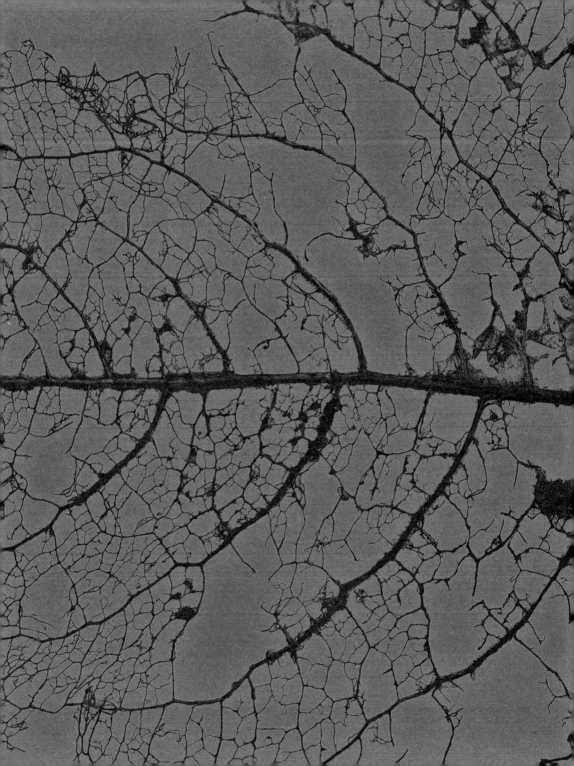